Printed in the USA

55 Great Ways
To Surprise Her

By Britt Sanders

Contents

When was the last time you treated your sweetie to something slightly more romantic than seats on the 50-yard line at an enormous stadium filled with beer-spilling, hot dog-wolfing fans? You try to show your love, consideration and thoughtfulness in meaningful ways, but for most men, wielding Cupid's bow and arrow on their own means missing the mark more often than not — usually by a long-shot. Some men will try to remedy the situation, but a quick search on the Internet for "romantic ideas" can lead to rather vague results, like broad, general suggestions for date nights or "duh" notions, such as holding the door for her. Is that how you want to show your significant other that you care? With tepid, been-there-done-that dates or ubiquitous acts of chivalry?

No, what you really want is to make a habit out of truly romantic gestures, acts that prove you are in tune with both her desires and your own capability for passion. Embracing that side of yourself might not come naturally to all men, which is why it's more than okay to get a little back-up in the name of wooing (or re-wooing) the one you love. This guide is filled to the brim with specific ideas that will make her heart flutter and her knees weaken, and if you want to take credit for it all by yourself — we won't tell on you!

Enduring relationships take work to keep the spice alive, and what matters more than anything is that you are asserting yourself to make her happy — by stoking the fires of romance through delightful surprises that offer more than a hint of excitement.

Before we get ahead of ourselves, though, we should start with a general introduction to relationships so that everyone is on the same page. With this book, it doesn't matter if you've only been coupled up for a few weeks or if you're looking at a 20-year wedding anniversary — what counts is that you are committed to both the one you love and the idea that you would do anything to make your relationship a satisfying one!

Keeping Relationship Fresh/Romantic

Being in a fun, positive, beneficial, nurturing, and loving relationship is one of the greatest joys in life but promoting long term success requires work. Many times couples end up breaking up because they lose the spice and freshness of the relationship and resort to a boring, predictable, stale existence. This trend does not have to define couples and one does not have to become a statistic. A boyfriend that is an adventurous, romantic, authoritative leader and a girlfriend that is a respectful, seductive, and fun lady may be more desirable than someone who is boring and argumentative. Here are 55 tips to help relationships not only survive, but thrive and these include recommendations on sex, romance, dates, adventures, finances, communication and more. Keeping the small things in mind and going the extra mile to keep a boyfriend or girlfriend happy will in turn make the other happy. A relationship is like most things of importance in that it needs attention and energy to keep it functioning properly. These concepts are effective for relationships that are relatively new to long term marriages.

Sexual Tips = Sex and sexual satisfaction is an important aspect of a relationship and many times a boring or stale relationship has a boring or stale sex life.

1. Role Playing - Sometimes the typical routine becomes boring in the bedroom and role playing can help add some excitement. The daily routine may become predictable and role playing can be a platform to make couples more comfortable, while being extra adventurous. A couple could play the role of cop and robber, doctor and nurse, or simply dominate and submissive. This can also be a fun night of acting and to make it more appealing, the entire endeavor can be recorded. The role playing can be extended outside of the bedroom; you can meet your mate at a bar or some other public place to help build up a night of passion. This tactic can be taken as seriously or as playfully as desired. This opportunity should be used to manifest characteristics that are fun exaggerations of thoughts and fantasies that cross the mind. This should be a top initial consideration when attempting to spice up the sex life.

2. Erotic Games - Many times couples do not put proper time and effort into foreplay and building up sexual energy and tension before the release. Fast forwarding a movie to the last 30 minutes to watch the climax will make it less enjoyable without seeing the incline that leads up to that point. One is more engaged and invested in the journey when they ride it from the beginning and erotic games can assist with this. Most erotic games promote arousal and foreplay, while incorporating actual fun and this helps gets the blood rushing to perhaps enjoy a better night of passion. These

games exist in many forms such as board, card, verbal, and more. Many involve performing acts on your partner or seductive conversation. Some couples are more private, but if comfort exists to play these games with other couples, it may be that much more fun. For example a game of strip poker with 4 people or two couples may be more engaging.

3. Different Routine - Some people find comfort with routine and the predictability of being a creature of habit. Others like to try new things and not knowing what's going to happen next. Many times these two types of people are in a relationship together and this can create a problem. One person thinks that the sex life and routine is great and the other is bored. If one has the "if it's not broke, don't fix it" mentality, that's fine but switch the routine from time to time to keep things spicy. This could involve a different location, positions, accessories, or even just temperament. If the lovemaking is normally slow and sensual, be rough sometimes and vice versa if applicable.

4. Erotic Movies - Watching erotic movies are a great catalyst for foreplay or simply an entertaining evening of viewing pleasure. Pornographic movies comes in all types and there is a niche that will surely cater to even the most specialized taste. Watching these could bring the couple closer together and spark ideas to implement into their own sex lives. This modern age makes unlimited types of videos available through the internet

and other forms of media where anyone can enjoy from the comfort of their own home. A nice interactive way to enjoy these movies is to somewhat mimic what actors are doing onscreen to add a special level of unpredictability. If erotic movies are already part of the relationship, a different type could help bring freshness. For those who don't and are hesitant to engage in porn, attempt a more sensual soft-core movie with script and storyline that will gradually introduce the erotica.

5. Bondage- The success of the "50 Shades of Grey" franchise is partly because it tapped into a deep primal almost subconscious desire for some women to be submissive. It is natural for a woman to want to be feminine and be with a man who can be dominant, masculine, and able to take what they want. Elements of bondage and control can help spice up the bedroom and enhance the overall dominate/submissive dynamic of the relationship or provide a refreshing reversal in the bedroom. When engaging in certain aspects of this, couples should set boundaries and have safety words to ensure everyone is at ease; although going outside the comfort zone is primarily the point. Handcuffs, rope, blindfolds, and perhaps some role playing can be incorporated into this. If a couple is comfortable with imploring paddles or whips into the mix, they may want to give it a try.

6. Lights, Camera, Action- It was mentioned that utilizing porn may be a great tool to not only keep the

sex life fresh but the entire relationship. To take it to another level, being active participants in making a personal home movie may be even more desirable. This can add many elements of teamwork and communication during the process of making something that is enjoyable; during and afterwards. Other elements can be combined with this such as role playing, bondage, and alterations to the routine without the camera. The end product is often a priceless irreplaceable window into time during a moment when passion is at it's best and this can be enjoyed years or decades to come. In the past, one had to spend additional money on expensive recording equipment to make a home video, but now almost every smart phone, tablet, and laptop contains a video recorder and making magic on the screen is the push of a button away.

7. Improve Skills- Like the old saying goes "there is always room for improvement" and even if one thinks they are god's gift to women/men and perform like a star in the bedroom, they should consider ways to enhance the pleasure of their mate and even themselves. For example, guys can perhaps take more interest in more stamina and movement to stimulate their girlfriend more. Women could learned advanced foreplay skills to blow their partner's mind and he will appreciate her interest in his pleasure. Having a nonchalant and content approach to the bedroom in a relationship can easily lead to disaster. People especially shouldn't dismiss their

partner if they are communicating dissatisfaction in the bedroom. Typically they aren't being needy and talking about pettiness, they are reaching out on a potentially deal breaking issue in an attempt to salvage a relationship that is headed toward an expiration date.

8. Phone Sex - This can be useful and a playful tactic before someone sees their mate later that day or as a tool to ease being apart for extended amounts of time. Focusing on the body during sex is natural but the sensual seductive side of sexuality is in large part mental, and verbal phone sex can better indulge in this side than being physically together sometimes. Furthermore, many times phone conversations with couples can be associated with being dull, quick, combative and such; and implementing romance and seductiveness with phone conversations can improve overall communication. This type of conversation can be completely just verbal and dirty talk or can involve participants being physical with themselves. For those even more adventurous, perhaps calling a professional erotic phone operator together can take it to another level.

9. Strange Places - Nothing is wrong with the bed and nothing is wrong with the bedroom, but there are other places to be intimate. Many times these different locations bring an element of taboo that gives an extra rush of excitement. The extra adventurous may consider things like public places and those people may consider

in the car parked somewhere, an empty movie theater, or outside at a deserted picnic or beach. The more conservative can still utilize this tip to keep things fresh as well. Even staying within the home, different locations can still be used. The living room couch, shower, kitchen, or backyard may all be locations to consider. Periodically and for no reason, getting a hotel room in or out of town for a night of passion might be the ideal change of scenery as well.

Romantic Tips = Keeping a romantic infatuation with your partner is just as important as sexual happiness and stimulates the mind and soul more.

10. Gifts for no Reason - Of course most people expect a gift on birthdays, Christmas, Valentines, and anniversaries, but the random gifts for no reason many times stand out more. A gift on those holidays is like doing the minimum job requirement for a position and that doesn't warrant much recognition, award, or extra cool points. A way to increase romanticism and make your mate feel like everyday is a holiday is to surprise them with a gift for no reason other than you love them. This approach doesn't have to be expensive as these types of gifts often are more about the thought, but don't be too frugal when it comes to promoting happiness in your life. Something like fresh flowers, shoes, or chocolate may be ideal for her and a watch, cologne, or a hat ideal for him. This gives the impression that the giver

is actively involved, appreciative, and interested in their mate and that can mean very much to some people.

11. Remember Anniversaries - It is generally accepted that women care more about anniversaries than men do but this isn't always true. It gives a nice gesture to imprint the date that a couple meets or became serious as it suggests that was a monumental day in life. A conversation about this date should be had before one flips out if it' forgotten but once it's established, it should be honored. Perhaps a celebration for each additional month into the relationship isn't warranted, but a six month and then annual anniversary can be special. Celebrating the anniversary can involve gifts, dates, vacations/trips, or just a special evening of reflection and plans for the future. Wedding anniversaries may hold even more significance after that step is taken and getting into the habit of appreciating less significant anniversaries is beneficial.

12. Promise/Engagement Ring - A way to keep the relationship fresh once it's established that you're with a keeper is to make a commitment. A relationship can fizzle out even in the mist of love if the partners aren't comfortable with the perceived devotion of their significant other. Communicating this commitment and having a symbol of it can strengthen the resolve for your girlfriend or boyfriend. The natural graduation from dating is being in a committed relationship and this can simply be verbally discussed and agreed or accompanied

with a ring. A promise ring may seem cheesy to some but you can give a simple random gift of jewelry that proceeds an engagement ring. Many guys are confident that they're with the love of their life but still hesitate to commit to the next level and this can stagnate and make stale a relationship very quickly. Ladies should not take their boyfriend reaching out for more commitment lightly and should embrace such acts of endearment if they desire to keep him around. This goes vice versa as either party can initiate more commitment or even propose.

13. Private Calendar - Many people still use a calendar to schedule events, mark birthdays, and simply view everyday. Giving a calendar to a partner as a gift with a special picture of yourself for each month can be a very romantic and seductive token. It will keep the boyfriend or girlfriend on each others mind and studies show this can promote favorable chemistry and emotion for the respective person. These pictures can be specialized for the seasons and holidays of each month or have a personal niche to it. The pictures can also be anything from G to X rated depending on the situation and location of the calendar. Personalized gifts like this touch the heart more and may be slightly more ideal for a girlfriend to give to a boyfriend, but can work reversed as well. A picture in a bathing suit wrapped in the US flag for July or in an erotic Santa suit for December seem

like appropriate classy and seductive themes for the calendar.

14. Cruise - Taking a cruise is a fun and adventurous endeavor for anyone regardless if they went alone, as a couple, with a group of friends, or with an entire family reunion. However, taking a cruise with your boyfriend or girlfriend is especially romantic and intimate. Many typical and economic cruises go to the Caribbean Islands and other exotic locations for 3 days to a week. This time together is spent eating gourmet meals, engaging in unlimited entertainment on the ship, breathtaking views of the oceans and island landscapes, visiting different cultures and more. The cabins and sleeping quarters have a nice ambiance and atmosphere and open balconies are available. These types of trips make lifetime memories and will surely keep any relationship fresh. The first trip may turn into a recurring tradition and there are many options and destinations to enjoy. The feeling of you and your mate on a ship of strangers and going to a foreign land where you probably don't know anyone gives a very romantic and adventurous "us against the world" feeling.

15. Jewelry - The old saying is that "diamonds are a girls best friend" and that can be partly true. Gold, silver, platinum, and precious gems have been not only highly desired for ages, it is the worlds oldest form of currency. If jewelry is purchased right, it is a easily liquid investment that can also be worn to enhance fashion and

appearance. Jewelry can last through generations and wearing it on the person constantly reminds the person of it's presence and origin. This is a very romantic gesture to give to your partner for these reasons and more. Typically it is not the cheapest gift but has origin of representing how royal your partner is and makes you feel. It is reminiscent of offering gold and diamonds to the queen or king. Guys appreciate jewelry as well and typically prefer gold chains, signet style rings, and designer watches. Females may have a preference for earrings, bracelets, and charmed necklaces.

16. Do A Chore - Sometimes doing a responsibility of your mates for them is the sweetest gesture and it gives them time, rest, and more peace of mind. This may be easier to do if the couple is living together but the act be even more appreciated if they don't. If the one partner typically cooks or does certain house cleaning, surprise them with it being done. This not only gives them time and rest as mentioned, but more importantly it shows them that you care! Not feeling appreciated and adored is a recipe for disaster in a relationship and kind gestures such as these promote an atmosphere of constantly adapting and doing for each other, which will in turn always help to keep things fresh. An easy gesture for one to do that doesn't live with their partner is to bring them lunch at work or run errands for them.

17. Pictures - In the beginning and after longevity is gained in a relationship, taking pictures together capture

important moments. Gazing these pictures and traveling down memory lane can be a reminder of the good times when things seem slow or stale. This reminder can be the catalyst to put forth effort in other areas mentioned to keep things fresh. This can be anything from taking selfies together to having high grade pictures taken by a professional photographer. Taking pictures of daily activities and fun can be great memories of the typical day and pictures on trips and special occasions are even more memorable. As time passes, periodic pictures can be like a timeline demonstrating where the relationship has come from and what it's endured. Video can be incorporated with pictures as well to create memories that are not only romantic and sentimental but priceless.

18. Massages - A sensual massage can be very intimate, romantic, and sexual and give legitimate muscle relaxation and stress relief to the recipient. This can be a mutually beneficial act as it allows the giver to know their partners body more and give sensual pleasure to them as well. These massages can be specialized and focused to trouble areas for the one receiving, such as the feet or the shoulders. Full body massages can be even more engaging and done purely as therapeutic or incorporated into the sex life. An appropriate time may be when a loved one gets off work, during a hot bubble bath, or right before bed. A couple that has a harmony of being in tune as one have a union of mind, body, and soul and massaging each other promotes body.

19. Public Affection - Some couples have mixed positions and comfort levels with displaying certain amounts of public affection, but engaging sometimes sends a powerful message. The notion of telling someone " I love you and I don't care who knows" is romantic but also sends a notion of priority. People have different levels of how much they care about what other people think, particularly strangers in public. Surely the opinion of one's beloved matters more than that of strangers and public affection can showcase this. The couple that excessively makes out inappropriately making others uncomfortable isn't exactly the model to follow. Subtle acts such as holding hands while walking, brief kisses, and even eye gazing can display to your partner that your affection doesn't have an on and off button that's dependent on who's watching.

20. Cook Together - Cooking for your partner can be romantic in itself, particularly a special meal that they love or a new recipe that you're proud of, but cooking together can be even more engaging and romantic. This type of cooperative act with a shared goal can bring parties closer together and promote good communication. Working in a close quartered hot and steamy kitchen can get the blood and hormones flowing. Keeping the relationship fresh can incorporate cooking fresh meals and the journey is just as good as the destination. The destination being enjoying a hopefully delicious meal that the couple made together, as a team,

which should be symbolic of how most endeavors are treated by the couple. Reaching a joint agreement on the dish to make and alternating who decides is a great way to include both people in the process.

21. Wash Together - There is something traditionally romantic about taking a shower or hot bubble bath with your mate. When people become one in a relationship, they often eat together, sleep together, play together, and it seems appropriate to also wash together sometimes. Of course this is a time when many appreciate privacy and alone time to relax so joint showers may not become the norm. Some couples may wash together on any given morning and not give it much thought and some may plan it and treat it as a scheduled honeymoon. In either case, it can have conscience and subconscious benefits of closeness. Besides washing yourself while in the tub or shower with your mate, taking turns washing each other in a sensual way is even more enjoyable. Laying together in a hot bubble bath until the water gets cool or relaxing in a hot tub with champagne can be a very romantic night.

22. Tattoos - A tattoo can be a long term display of affection and should not be taken lightly. Many times you'll see a young couple with names tattooed on various parts of each others body and sometimes it's seen as tactless but it can be classy and romantic. Getting this type of tattoo shouldn't be a spur of the moment thing or done with someone you aren't completely serious about

being with long term. This can be as big an obligation as a promise or engagement ring and should be done in good faith. It's even more romantic if both parties get tattoos at the same time. The tattoos can be simply getting each others name or getting more platonic matching tattoos that has a special meaning or relation to the relationship. For example, it has been trending for finances and married couples to get matching tattoos around their ring finger.

Communication = Proper communication can turn a potential deal breaker scenario into a valuable lesson learned and strengthen the relationship.

23. Talk About Issues - When issues and problems arise in a relationship, it can be almost natural for some to avoid or suppress the subject. Keeping emotions bottled inside can allow them to fester, worsen, and explode in a moment of anger that can be very detrimental to the relationship. Open lines of communication puts the couple in a position that allows symptoms of root causes to be better diagnosed and handled. If boredom is the direct issue, then communicating this and reaching resolutions is what can simultaneously save the relationship and make it more exciting. Communication, even when dealing with disagreements, should never be arguments, more so a debate if even that. Mutual respect is important when talking about sensitive issues and couples should refrain from name calling, yelling, sarcastic/condescending

tones, and other offensive tactics. Remember, that you and your mate should be cooperative and not competitive so a heated conversation is not an attempt to see who can out wit or disrespect the other more. A conversation should be an attempt to resolve the issue at hand and not create a bigger issue out of how the root cause is addressed.

24. Honesty - The old saying that "honesty is the best policy" is very true and deceitful lies can make a fresh relationship stale very fast. It is hard to regain trust after being labeled a liar and lies get old very fast. Being with someone that is honest and trustworthy is often one of the first and primary qualities that most people look for in a mate. Once this is demonstrated to me non-existent, most people will leave the situation then or give the relationship an expiration date. Once it's realized that someone is not an ideal life partner, things get stale fast as the overall effort to make other facets of the relationship work goes out the window. Keeping secrets and lying to your significant other is like keeping things from yourself or having multiple personalities, it's insane. One should trust their boyfriend or girlfriend with many things and this is only escalated after things like kids, living together, and marriage comes into play. It should be natural and comfortable to trust your mate with secrets, money, safety, faithfulness, and more. How can anyone take someone serious and be vulnerable by opening up to them if they can't even be trusted.

25. Loyalty/Faithfulness - Loyalty and faithfulness goes in hand with honesty and all are important to the success of a couple. A simple tip in this arena is just to be loyal and faithful to the partner in a relationship and make it easy for them to give the same in return. If someone in the couple is not being faithful, they aren't even in a real relationship, but simply engaging in deceit and espionage. Someone cheating on a mate is similar to cheating themselves out of a potential long term and loving relationship. It's not healthy and brings negative energy to all those involved. If someone is not ready for a committed relationship then they should not enter one and simply have a life of casual sex, one night stands, and booty calls. That life is shallow and gets old fast as it only addresses the physical need for a companion but does little to nothing for the yearning for a mental, emotional, and spiritual connection with someone. Loyalty also includes simple things like taking up for your mate when they're not present and prioritizing who's most important in your life.

26. Discuss Gender Roles - Many times conflicts within a relationship arise because there is no proper discussion of expectations and compatibility. This is a bad foundation for good communication moving forward. Discussing gender roles includes more than discussing who's the expected breadwinner and if the female will be a stay at home mom. It often times involves fighting for dominance in the relationship.

Most guys don't want to get into a challenge or confrontation with their girlfriend over who's going to be the alpha male in the relationship. If a guy wanted to be with a guy, he'd probably would be; many men can appreciate a feminine woman more than a masculine one. A woman than has a feminine and submissive temperament would be compatible with a different type of man than an aggressive one that likes to wear the pants in the relationship. On the flip side, a more passive soft spoken man may not be macho enough for a woman than needs strong leadership. Good communication helps shine light on these issues before time and energy is invested into a relationship that is doomed to fail.

27. Don't Be Jealous - It can be flattering for someone to know that other people want or desire their mate but jealousy can arise as well. There is nothing wrong with being a little territorial with your mate and it actually shows them that you care, but intense jealousy can be a little disturbing. If a mate gives you reason to be jealous then jealousy isn't the root cause and perhaps the mate being inappropriate or acting untrustworthy is the root cause. That is a separate issue and warrants action, but someone being jealous for no reason or over reacting needs to resolve internal issues within themselves. People should be able to trust their mate's loyalty, and faithfulness if it is present. Advise a mate if any of their actions are borderline inappropriate rather than being jealous and not addressing root cause. Jealousy can hint

at insecurity and this is unattractive if it's excessive and unwarranted and can make the other person feel clustered and make the relationship stale.

28. Social Media - Sites such as Facebook, Twitter, Instagram, and others have not only changed how the world communicates but directly affects relationships as well. Some people have more of an online and social media presence than others so this issue is not universal. For others, social networking sites are a source of infidelity, jealousy, a web to get caught in lies, and a premise for arguments. Many dilemmas revolve around acting single or inappropriate online profile content and comments. Communicating with old flames online or flirting with cyber friends has been the source for much turmoil for couples in recent years. Don't let a issue that was non-existent in the recent past be the sabotage to a potential life long union with the love of your life. For example, prematurely changing a relationship status to single on Facebook after an argument with your boyfriend/girlfriend can be a rush to act and be the nail in the coffin to a relationship that could have been salvageable.

Dates = Date nights are very symbolic of the current nature and happiness of a relationship and it can grow couples closer together.

29. Camping - Camping in the woods doesn't have to be an experience like on the show "Naked and Afraid". It

can be a fun, romantic, and adventurous endeavor that brings the couple closer together and with nature. A couple being alone, just the two of them in the wilderness and dependent on each other is potentially romantic and has a primal survivor element to it. Just focusing on each other with no television, technology, neighbors, or distractions can be refreshing. This type of date is economic and very memorable and is a nice change of pace for those not accustom to it and is a comfortable getaway for those who are. Holding each other while sitting by the fire, cuddling in a sleeping bag, or even going skinny dipping in a lake can add positive energy to almost any relationship. This could even be a group event with some friends being invited for the trip as well.

30. Beach - The beach has long been a location for great summer fun for friends, family, couples, and individual beach bums alike. There is something unique and refreshing about where the sea meets land, the sand underneath the feet, sound of waves crashing, smell of the ocean, and the peaceful ambiance. This also allows you to see each other in sexy beachwear and swimsuits and can increase libido. An all day event with grilling food, coolers full of beer, volleyball, music, and invited friends can be just what the doctor ordered to add some freshness to the relationship when the summer time arrives. A private type location on the beach with just the two of you can be special as well and more intimate.

Night time visits to the beach can be especially romantic and adventurous and the brave may engage in extra raunchy activity like skinny dipping or fooling around on the beach.

31. Amusement Park - The amusement park is not only for kids as adults can have even more fun. Running around a big amusement park like a kid with the one you love is a truly magical and memorable time. It's almost like Peter Pan and Wendy running and flying around Neverland. All of the activities from the roller-coasters, water parks, games, food, live shows, and other attractions are well more than enough to keep the itinerary full. Taking the special park pictures, yelling while facing the perils of the dissension of skyscraper high coasters, lounging in the lazy river, and the other specialized couple activities are sure to add spice to the sometimes typical serious dread of everyday grown up life. Perhaps a great end to an extravagant day at the amusement park reliving your second childhood is to spend the night having adult fun.

32. Live Music - Great music can be great entertainment and the foundation for a great night on the town with a significant other. Jamming to music in the car, at the house, and in the club is nice, but there is nothing like seeing a favorite performer live or even sampling local underground entertainment. Listening to live music that is sensual and about love such as certain pop, r&b, or even instrumental jazz/classical music can

be romantic and hearing live allows it to imprint more. Hearing a beautiful voice singing live about being in love while you sit with your loved one and eye gazing can be a very special and deep moment that can brings closeness and ignites appreciation. It helps remind you of why you're together and help put verbalization to how you feel. Even instrumental music can create that romantic ambiance that is a nice fresh change of pace from the mindless noise that pollutes much of the airwaves.

33. Sauna Night - There are private sauna locations in many major cities and these are ideal places to have a different type of date to add freshness to a relationship. These are steam rooms that allow customers to go in toweled or naked for relaxation and holistic detox. This is a great atmosphere to go with your partner to relax and get closer. It allows for silent peaceful rest in a very different atmosphere or can be the ideal location for deep conversations. In a sense, a sauna is a great place to detoxify not just the body but also the mind/soul by discussing and resolving festering issues in the relationship. Many of these locations also feature hot tubs with open roofs that allow couples to star gaze and enjoy the night sky while relaxing in the bubbling water. That atmosphere can be especially enjoyed on a cool spring or fall night.

34. Drive in Movie - These type of movie theaters are not extinct although it may be an endangered species. Drive in movies are still existent in most parts of the

country and almost present in at least every state. Not only is this type of date night like a blast from the past and reminiscent perhaps of how parents and grandparents courted but it eliminates many of the complaints of traditional movie theaters. These complaints are that you can't talk, no privacy, too crowded, potentially unsafe, and more. Being in the privacy of your own vehicle and viewing a popular new movie in a car amidst a parking lot of other couples in love is very probably to ignite sparks in the relationship. Many times, movie goers aren't even able to attentively finish the movie because things become so hot and romantic inside the vehicle, hence this is a great tactic to keep things fresh.

35. Play Sports - Playing sports against your mate may seem like a recipe for disaster for those who are already too competitive, but it can be a fun activity to spice things up. The first sport that comes to mind to play with your mate is basketball. This is a popular team sport that can be played one on one and requires close contact that can be turned sensual when playing a girlfriend or boyfriend. Sports like football, baseball, soccer, and hockey would not be ideal, primarily because of the needed participants. Besides basketball, other sports to consider would be tennis, golf, bowling, or simply exercising together. Other less physical activities could be playing pool, video games, cards, or pin pong. Play wrestling may also be desired by some because it's

playful competition that can be refreshing and help remove the competitiveness that exists in everyday life with some couples.

36. Double Date - Going on a date to any location with your mate can be special but there is a special atmosphere and dynamic when it's a group event. Double dating is a great tactic to use when wanting to add spice and a different type of excitement to date night. Having multiple people there and witnessing your boyfriend/girlfriend in social situations with others can help you appreciate their great personality more. This realization can make you truly realize the great catch that you have and want them that much more. This gives an opportunity for entertainment that includes more than just you two and makes the time alone even more valuable. A double date can be anything from a dinner and movie, to miniature golf, to playing cards at the house. If a couple has mutual friends that are a couple this is even more appropriate and married couples that have married friends should be even more engaged in double dates.

37. Horror and Chick Flick Movies - Movies are one of the oldest past times in modern history for an entertaining evening alone, coupled up, or with family and friends. Even going to the movie theaters is perhaps the most cliche type of date to go on. This doesn't mean it's not a way to add freshness to a relationship or that it's expendable. Watching a good movie together for the

first time is like going on a trip without leaving your seat. Many genres can suffice in this type of date including action, drama, and thrillers but horror and romantic comedy movies seem to be the most applicable for a date night, particularly at home. Horror movies intend to ignite fear and this in turns makes movie watchers extra clingy and appreciative of the partner in life they have. It reminds them that they wouldn't have to go through such horrific events alone. Romantic comedies or chick flicks combine comedy that may appeal more to him and romance that may appeal more to her and is a way to appreciate your probable normal/stable relationship compared to the spectacle that was likely on screen.

Finances = One of the main reasons that couples argue and break up is related to money and financial woes, prepare for this and make it irrelevant to the relationship's survivability.

38. Budget - Sticking to a budget is important when you're single but even more important when in a serious relationship. The concept of being one with your mate involves making decisions together and realizing you are not only spending your money, but spending the foundation to potentially build a family with. Arguments of unnecessary purchases and limited funds can be addressed by a pre-established system of spending money. If one partner spends most their money on wants, then necessities and bills become the burden of the other person. Depending on the situation, this isn't

fair and is the premise for conflict. Money is the most relevant aspect of survivability in the modern age and should be treated as such. A long time ago when we were hunters and gathers, a mates desirability was largely determined by how well they could hunt and gather because choosing a mate was as serious as choosing someone who best promotes you surviving. Now, the ability to make and properly spend money is the equivalent of this and still speaks to desirability of and survival instinct of people searching for a mate.

39. Discuss Goals - An important aspect of communication is discussing goals and this helps eliminates any future aspirations that aren't feasible for the couple as a whole and is a constant reminder of what is being worked toward. This constant reminder of things to come is a natural refresher and reminds that there are greater things in the future of the relationship. The goals discussed should be short term, long term, personal, for the couple, and a potential family. Discussing goals also promotes a nature and habit of better communication in regards to many other issues. Transparency and being an open book with your partner ensures that everyone is on the same page and anything less is an omission of information that could be considered deceit. If someone in the relationship is unaware of or hasn't considered any goals of the future, then the bigger issue is an epiphany and realization of these goals.

40. Start Part Time/Small Business Together - Making money together and starting a business addresses several key issues for a couple. It helps address financial problems and it promotes more quality time together. The communication that is required to make a business function together is symbolic of making the relationship work, raising kids, or running a household together. A small part time endeavor at the flea market over the weekend or running a website together could be the right amount of change and newness to the relationship. This takes the relations further from just being a couple or life partners to being business partners and this further entangling of lives can strengthen the bond. Too much money can never be had and the extra funds generated from this opportunity can allow for payment of stress causing bills or to take a romantic getaway.

41. Discuss Big Purchases - Many often forget when they are in a serious relationship that they are part of a team and many selfish or individual primary concerns are juggled with what's best for the unit. Big purchases that aren't sanctioned by a partner in a relationship are one of the leading causes for financial turmoil. Communication about these issues does not have to be seen as asking permission, but simply a discussion to seek their counsel on the subject. This shows them that you value their opinion and the financial obligations of the couple before personal aspirations. This also

showcases financial responsibility, which is an important trait that one looks for in a spouse. To show your mate that you are long term material and a keeper, be financially responsible. Everyone deserves to treat themselves and splurge sometimes, but a habit of non-discussed personal extravagant purchases to the detriment of the financial health of the couple is a deal breaker for many if not at least a cause for tension.

42. Become Roommates - If the boyfriend and girlfriend lives apart, moving in together can have many positive effects for them. However, this shouldn't be done as a method to salvage an already bad relationship, but as a means to move a stagnate one to the next level. Living with someone allows a chance to truly get to know the everyday them and could reveal any potential deal breakers earlier or it'll bring the couple closer together, either has benefits. This is a strong move that shows a relationship is truly serious and on the most adult level. Besides the positive ramifications on the quality and freshness added to the relationship by living together, it presents strong financial benefit as well. A couple moving in together that each has their own apartments will be able to greatly reduce monthly bills and expenses. This practicality is a strong premise and reason for serious relationships to begin with.

43. Carpool - Driving to work together can save gas and potentially eliminate the need for a second vehicle, which will generate even more savings. The time

commuting in a vehicle is where some of the most deep and relevant conversations happen for people in general, including couples. This time promotes communication and closeness that may be non-existent if not sitting in a car and being unable to walk to the next room or hang up the phone. Some may find annoyance in having to get picked up or not having a vehicle nearby for an unexpected emergency, but others find it refreshing to have their knight or their heroine pick them up from a long day of hard work. The ride home may also increase the likelihood of spontaneous stops and adventures that would otherwise never happen.

Quality Time = One of the major reasons for being in a relationship is not to feel lonely; feeling neglected can lead partners astray.

44. Scheduled Time Apart - In a relationship it can feel natural to want to spend every woken and sleeping moment with your beloved, however everyone needs some alone and personal time. People in relationships having alone time to themselves just to think, reflect, and indulge in privacy and personal time to perhaps company friends and family members is often necessary. Smoldering or handcuffing your mate can have an adverse effect that drives them away. Your mate should feel like you are a magnet that draws them near; an energy that they don't want to be away from. This feeling should not morph into a feeling of a prisoner needing to escape. If a couple lives apart then many times the issue

is more so spending enough time together, but for those living together, time apart may be a more relevant issue. Time apart can make one appreciate who they have home waiting for them even more and promotes quality time over just quantity time.

45. Spend Adequate Time Together - Feeling lonely while you're in a relationship is like always being broke when you have a full time job, it shouldn't happen. It's natural for someone feeling a void of loneliness to seek to have that void filled elsewhere if their mate is doing an inadequate job. Even if a boyfriend or girlfriend seems ok with a difficult schedule and rarely seeing each other, the busy one should go out their way to see the other more. This is especially true if they have bend patient and understanding for a period of time already, as more time together should be there reward. Taking someone's patience and kindness for granted and weakness is a common mistake that leads to unexpected breakups. A wise person always makes time for what's important and if a significant other is truly significant, they should be treated like it. Once spending time with your partner seems like a chore you procrastinate to do, there is trouble in paradise.

46. Lay up - "Laying up" is a term used to described casually laying in bed with your partner for an extended amount of time. Someone can be laid up with their partner all day at home on a mutual day off or all evening and night at a hotel out of town. If the

relationship is sexual, the general census is that every couple should spend enough time being laid up as it's romantic, sexual, and very intimate. A typical laid up day can include a toggling of laying in bed talking, watching television, sex, napping, eating in bed, and cuddling/eye gazing. Simply sleeping together at night or being in bed together exclusively for sex doesn't constitute laying up because as mentioned, it's more than just that. A couple should set aside adequate time to just lay in bed, do nothing, and enjoy each other for hours on end. Some couples even lay up all weekend or for an entire vacation and that seems to be refreshing, particularly if it's long overdue.

47. Periodic Dates - Considering the type of date to take is one conversation but simply deciding to have any date at all is another. Many couples procrastinate and put dates on the back burner and this isn't healthy for the relationship. To put having a date on the back-burner excessively is like putting each other on the back-burner. Prioritizing and taking time out to work on and keep the relationship fresh by going out is a remedy for the couples who grow tired of sitting home every weekend night playing video games or staring in each other faces. Besides the ones who don't find the time, there are those who minimize the importance of such outings and deemed them as unnecessary. This is even more troubling as the procrastinator may eventually prioritize, but the ones dismissive of dates may be down

a path of a lifetime of boring and stale relationships or loneliness.

48. Meet the Family - To meet the family of your girlfriend or boyfriend can be a daunting task and even intimidating for some. The desire to ensure you impress with a great first impression can be overwhelming pressure but it should be looked at in a positive light. Most people don't introduce casual dates or insignificant people in their lives to their family as it would be too many introductions. The opportunity to meet them should be valued and reinforce the fact that you and your mate are serious and moving up to the next level. Most families are reasonable people and thrilled at the fact that someone is making their loved one happy. Be open to introduce your partner to your family when the time is right and communicate how you're open to meeting theirs as well. Many families have fun and engaging family culture and this experience will likely be memorable and without many dull moments.

Take Care of Yourself = Don't assume because you have your fish already hooked that it's impossible for them to go anywhere. Maintain the excellence that first attracted them because that is the person they fell for.

49. Stay in Shape - It has become almost a cliche for many to think that after a person gets in a serious relationship or gets married, that they will let themselves go and get fat and ugly. This isn't the case for many but

for some it does have some relevance. It is common for people to have their best appearance when single as they are trying to attract a lover, but this same level of self pride in appearance should be maintained when in the relationship. Otherwise it could be compared to false advertisement or bait and hook. Appreciating a partner should mean staying fit and maintaining an ideal weight not just to get or remain attractive for them, but for your own health. Of course no one wants to be with a shallow and superficial person that is primarily concerned about looks but if you truly adore your lover, you should want to look as good as possible for them. Maintaining an ideal weight also promotes you both doing more active and adventurous outings. Going to the gym and exercising together is a great activity to spend quality time and keep fit and in shape together.

50. Dress Sexy When Appropriate - Don't go everywhere with your boyfriend or girlfriend with sweatpants and dirty sneakers or flip flops on. Take pride in your fashion and try to dress to impress when you go on a date and when appropriate. It doesn't have to be expensive to have a wardrobe of presentable clothes with sex appeal. Don't take it too far and dress like a hooker or male stripper from Magic Mike, but remind them why they're lucky to be with you.

51. Value Your Health - Typical marriage vows involve staying with each other during sickness and health and while this should be true, a person has a

responsibility not only to themselves, but to their mate to do everything possible to live a long healthy life. Going to the doctor regularly, exercising, eating healthy, avoiding drugs and poisons, and being preventive when it comes to health issues should go without saying. Being in a relationship with someone who is self destructive speaks volumes on that respective person's priorities and outlook. If someone doesn't love themselves enough to have self preservation, their partner may wonder "how can they love me".

52. Remember Hygiene - Nothing can spoil the moment more and make things stale quicker than bad hygiene, particularly during intimate moments. Men and women should take heed of this; cleanliness is next to godliness. People should attempt to be extra fresh and clean when around their boyfriend or girlfriend. Being freshly showered when first greeting, utilization of perfumes, colognes, lotions, and deodorant is necessary. Bad breath is one of the biggest enemies of kissing and close intimacy and breath mints or gum should be readily available in case a make-out session spontaneously arises.

53. Be Confident - There is nothing sexier than confidence and one should be especially confident around their mate. Confidence in appearance, decision making skills, and the strength of the relationship is more attractive than the most seductive strip tease. When a mate gets the impression that their partner is

insecure or weak, it typically goes one of two ways. They'll take advantage of the situation or they'll pity the person and both scenarios often lead to the relationship eventually ending. A significant other wants a strong person to represent them and a lack of confidence in their mate gives warranted reason for concern.

54. Wrap it Up/Get Checked Out - It is vital that safe sex is practiced to properly enjoy it so the concerns and worries of potential ramifications don't over shadow the pleasure. Condoms should be used in the beginning of a relationship to ensure that an unplanned pregnancy doesn't happen, to prevent STD's, and to vet the person further until you're confident in their faithfulness and trustworthiness. After issues such as this is vetted and another form of contraception is verified, papers can be provided to prove a clean bill of health, and there is mutual trust in monogamy, it may be considered then to go without.

55. Compliments - People often underestimate how powerful a simple and genuine compliment can be to the receiving person. Even a compliment from a stranger can completely make a person day. A legitimate compliment from a boyfriend or girlfriend carries even more value as most people care about the opinion of their mate more than anyone else. Good compliments can be about the physical, mental, work ethic, talents, morals, sexuality, or about anything that is truly appreciated. Making him or her feel appreciated gives

them extra energy to try to keep things fresh on their end and fight to ultimately stay together. Hopefully, If you're with someone, it's for good reason and telling them why before it's too late can make all the difference.

Conclusion

Many times the flame burning out in a passionate and loving relationship isn't the result of difficult circumstances or environment, but of a lack of effort to keep things fresh. A man should treat his woman like a queen and she should treat him like a king. If this utmost level of respect and devotion is given, the relationship is destined for greatness and longevity. The sex life should remain vibrant, communication should be strong, romance should flourish, looks should be kept up, and dates should be fun. Additionally, don't take the person you're with for granted; don't assume they aren't going anywhere because of an overestimation of their tolerance. And finally, remember that love is stronger than pride and there is nothing weak about conceding for the one you love when appropriate. Implement these tips in personal relations and constantly think of new ways to keep things fresh as everyone grows and changes as a person; so the efforts to keep relationships strong should as well.